BEATRICE HOLLYER has spent much of her time as journalist, writer, and newscaster. She began her media career in South Africa before moving to the UK, where she has lived for the past ten years. Today she works as a freelance writer and is the author of two parenting books. This is her first book for children.

TONY ROBINSON is an established television actor, presenter and writer. Famous for his role as Baldrick in *Blackadder*, his recent work includes the popular history series *Time Team*. He has also worked with Comic Relief and has been a supporter of Oxfam for many years.

FOR CLEMENTINE AND HER GRANDMAMA – B.H.

Wake Up, World!: A Day in the Life of Children Around the World
© Frances Lincoln Limited 1999

Text copyright © Frances Lincoln Limited 1999
Photographs copyright © Oxfam Activities Limited
and the photographers as named 1999

First published in 1999 by Frances Lincoln Limited,
4 Torriano Mews, Torriano Avenue, London NW5 2RZ

First paperback edition 1999

British Library Cataloguing in Publication Data
available on request.

ISBN 0-7112-1359-3 hardback
ISBN 0-7112-1484-0 paperback

Illustrations by Diane Lilley
Designer: Sarah Slack
Project Editor: Cathy Fischgrund,
Project Editor for Oxfam: Anna Coryndon

Printed in Hong Kong
5 7 9 8 6 4

Oxfam and the publishers would like to thank all the children who
took part in *Wake Up, World!*, and their families and communities for
their enthusiastic support. Oxfam commissioned photographers from
around the world to visit the eight children featured in the book and,
together with the publishers, would like to thank them:

Julio Etchart visited Ludovico village in Brazil to
meet Cidinha and her family.

Rajendra Shaw lives and works in Hyderabad,
India. He took the photographs of Shakeel.

Sarah Errington travelled to Western Siberia
to visit Sasha and his family, followed by a trip
to Ghana to Anusibuno's village.

Penny Tweedie took the photographs of Alexis
and her friends in Alice Springs, Australia.

Sean Sprague visited Natali at her home in
California, USA.

Jim Holmes took the photographs of Linh in
Ky Anh, Vietnam.

Howard Davies took the photographs of Paige
in Brighton, UK.

*Oxfam GB will receive a 5% royalty for each copy of this book sold in the UK.
Oxfam is a Registered Charity no. 202918. Oxfam GB is a member of Oxfam International.*

*Oxfam believes every human being is entitled to a life of dignity and opportunity. Working with others we use our
ingenuity, knowledge and wealth of experience to make resources and money work harder. From practical work
with individuals through to influencing world policy we enable the world's poorest people to create a future that
no longer needs Oxfam.*

Wake up, World!

A Day in the Life of Children Around the World

BEATRICE HOLLYER

Introduction by Tony Robinson

FRANCES LINCOLN in association with Oxfam

I have a friend called Cidinha who cracks a hundred nuts every day – they're the size of apples, with shells as hard as a very hard sum. They grow on trees around her village.

Cidinha is seven years old. You may think she's quite different from you – and I'm not just talking about the nut-cracking. Her house is made of mud and leaves. She sleeps in a hammock. She's never played a computer game or queued for a burger. So, she is very different from you, isn't she?

Well maybe, but maybe not. She has a gang of friends (just like you) who go to their own special places and tell each other secrets. She knows all the latest pop songs. She's sometimes picked on by her older brothers and sisters, and she doesn't think it's fair when she has to go to bed earlier than they do. All that's a bit like you, isn't it?

So why does she crack nuts? Well, everyone in her village does. Before Cidinha was born, farmers tried to drive her family and friends out of their village so that they could take over the land. Everyone was scared, but they stayed put and they stayed together. They wanted to make their lives better. Nuts grew all around them, so they set up a factory which uses oil from them to make soap that they can sell. Cidinha is proud of the soap factory. Nut-cracking is her part in making the village better.

In lots of ways Cidinha's life is very different from yours, but it's also similar. And that's true of children all over the world. We're going to tell you eight stories about children from all four corners of the globe. Some of their lives may seem a little strange to you, but remember there are some things we have in common. They all like to stay up late, they all like sweets, they all moan when they're not allowed to go out and play, and they all get told off about sixteen times a day. And that's definitely like you, isn't it?

Tony Robinson

My name is **PAIGE**. It was my grandmother's surname before she was married, and it's my mother's middle name. I live in Brighton in the **UNITED KINGDOM**.

My name is **NATALI** which means 'born at Christmas'. My middle name Xochiquetzal (zo-ki-kwet-zal) is the name of the Mexican Goddess of Spring. I live in Berkeley, California, in the **UNITED STATES OF AMERICA**.

My name is Aparecida (a-pa-re-thi-da) but everyone calls me **CIDINHA** (shid-jin-ya). I live in Ludovico village in **BRAZIL**.

My name is **ANUSIBUNO** (an-oo-si-boo-no) which means 'things of my hand'. I live in Zuo village in **GHANA**.

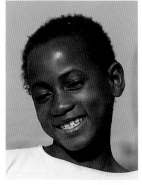

World

My name is **SASHA**. It is short for Alexandr which means 'winner'. I live in Lekarstvennoye village in **RUSSIA**.

My name is **LINH** (ling). We put our family names first, then our first names, so my full name is Hoang Xuan Linh (hon zu-an ling). I live in Ky Anh in **VIETNAM**.

My name is **ALEXIS**. My surname Abala is an Aboriginal name. I live in Alice Springs in **AUSTRALIA**.

My name is Mohammad Shakeel although everyone knows me as **SHAKEEL**. It means 'handsome'. I live in Hyderabad in **INDIA**.

Wake up!

The moment when we open our eyes
to a new day is something we all share.
But what we see, feel and hear around us
is different, depending on where we live.

"I like to sleep late in my hammock.
It's so comfortable that my mother has to
shake me awake. In the room where I sleep
we store rice in big sacks."—**Cidinha**

Alexis' house has four bedrooms.
Her room has bunk beds, and she sleeps in
the top bunk. After her mother wakes her,
she makes her bed before climbing down
for breakfast.

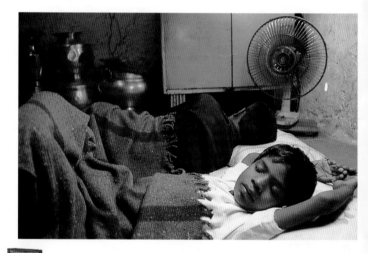

Shakeel and his brother Shabeer sleep until
their mother wakes them. Their bed is a mattress on
the floor. An electric fan blows cool air over them.

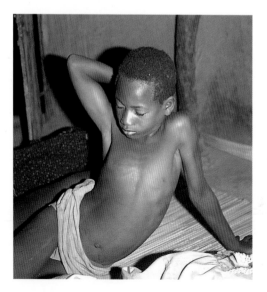

As she wakes up, Anusibuno stretches
on the sleeping mat she shares with her mother
and four sisters. When it's hot, they move the
mat and sleep outside.

 "It's dark and cold outside when I wake up. Our cat, Pushok, keeps me warm. He is like a fluffy blanket."—**Sasha**

 Natali wakes herself up with her alarm clock. Once she's awake, she reads or pretends her bed is a zoo, full of her toy animals.

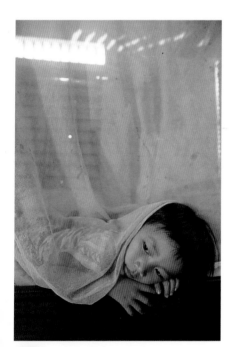

When Linh wakes up, he lifts the mosquito net that covers the bed he shares with his mother, father and brother. They sleep, eat and watch television in the same room.

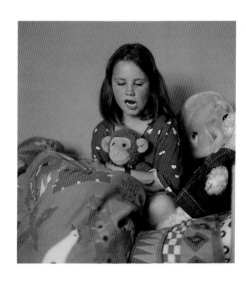

Paige cuddles her toy monkey as she gets up. Her bedroom is painted pink, her favourite colour. She likes to watch TV while her parents are still asleep.

Who else is awake?

When we wake up, we look around and see who else is up and about. We say, "Good morning!" to people and animals who share our homes. All over the world, children live with their parents, brothers and sisters, and sometimes grandparents, aunts, uncles or cousins. Pets and other animals are part of family life, too.

Before Shakeel wakes up, his mother fetches water from the tap on the road, so that he and his father can wash. Together they set up a small table and a mirror in the courtyard of their house. Shakeel brushes his teeth while he watches his father shave.

The pigs and chickens are waiting for their breakfast when Cidinha wakes up. Her mother has lit the stove, fetched water from the well and made coffee for everyone. She calls Cidinha to feed the animals. Her father and big brother have already left for work in the fields.

Alexis likes to see all her toys at the end of her bed. She pretends they are waiting for her to wake up. Her mother is busy getting her five brothers and sisters ready for school.

Every morning Sasha is up early, helping to dress his younger sister Yulya, and make breakfast. His stepfather is away working, so Sasha takes pride in being the man of the house, helping his mother and *babushka* (Russian for grandmother) in every way he can.

"My mother wakes up at dawn because she has so much to do before she starts work in the fields. Then my father gets up and goes to work, leaving lots of space in our family bed. My brother is still asleep when I start doing my homework."—**Linh**

★ Natali and her older sister Ali like to spend time together in the bathroom after they wake up, brushing their teeth, chatting and looking in the mirror. They sometimes forget that their parents and uncle also need to use the bathroom!

🏠 "I get up before everyone else and help myself to a drink, because I can't wait to start the day. If Mum and Dad are still asleep, my sister and I play with my hamster, Hamish. He's nocturnal, so he's been awake most of the night."—**Paige**

Anusibuno wakes up with her parents, four sisters and 24 other relations. They share a compound, a collection of rooms in a walled yard. Her father and the other men get up first, to let out the animals to graze in the open until night falls.

Starting the day

Between waking up and setting off for school, children across the globe eat breakfast, wash, brush their teeth and get dressed. In hot countries, we wake up with a quick splash of cool water, and pull on a pair of shorts. In cold climates, everything takes longer: no one wants to get out of a warm bed and then put on layers of clothes to brave the cold outside.

"I shower, dress, then help myself to breakfast - cereal, orange juice and yoghurt - which I eat with my sisters. My little brother is still asleep and my big brother has already left for school on his bicycle." When Alexis goes out, she has to remember to wear her hat, to protect herself from the burning sun.

Anusibuno washes in the water she has carried from the well. Afterwards, she rubs shea butter on to her skin, to protect it from the wind and sun. She would love to wear brightly-coloured clothes, but she has only one skirt and T-shirt which she wears every day for school. For breakfast, she eats *pumpuka*, millet porridge, sometimes with smoked fish and spices.

On school days, Paige prepares breakfast for herself and her sister. They have a choice of cereals, then toast with peanut butter. After breakfast, Paige brushes her teeth before deciding what to wear.

Sasha boils water for tea while his mother fries potatoes. For a treat, he sometimes has milk, and bread and butter for breakfast. Before he goes out in the snow, he puts on an extra sweater, padded jacket and trousers, felt boots, mittens, a scarf and a fur hat.

 "For breakfast, we eat *parathas*, bread fried in oil, and we drink tea - I add lots of sugar to mine! We eat in the courtyard, just outside the kitchen. Afterwards Ammy (Mummy) helps me get ready for school. I like wearing new clothes, and I look forward to festival days when we get clothes as presents."—**Shakeel**

Cidinha washes with soap made from babassu nuts. The water comes from a deep well. It still has some earth in it, but it's soft and cool. After her bucket shower, she has coffee mixed with manioc flour, made from the cassava plant. Breakfast is indoors because it's hot and dusty outside.

"I often wear my favourite sweater, handed down from Ali. The dogs on it remind me of my grandparents' dog, Farley. Ali lets me borrow her earrings and helps me to put them on. Once I'm dressed, I eat breakfast, usually toasted bagels and cereal."—**Natali**

After he's done his homework, Linh washes rice for his mother to cook with fish and vegetables for breakfast. When he's finished eating, he brushes his teeth, perched on the wall outside his house so that he can see what everyone else is up to.

Off to school!

When we go to school, we step outside our homes and families to a new place among children of our own age. Depending on where we live, we make the journey in different ways. For some of us, it's a long walk, with a chance to play along the way; others ride in a bus, train or car.

Natali's uncle walks her to school. When it rains, they go by car. After school starts, the gates are locked to keep the children safe.

"School is only two minutes away. It takes Mum longer to get us all into the car than it does to drive there!"—**Alexis**

Linh walks to school at midday when it is extremely hot. He always remembers his satchel, but sometimes he forgets his hat.

Anusibuno shares bags of nuts with her friends on their half-hour walk to school. They like to hang around the water-pump chatting, until the grown-ups shout, "Hurry or you'll be late!"

"I ride to school in my father's auto-rickshaw, a taxi with three wheels. I see lots of monkeys on the way."—**Shakeel**

"I walk to school alone. It's quiet and beautiful. I look at the different-coloured houses - red, yellow and green - and I see how beautiful they are."—**Sasha**

If it's wet, Paige goes to school by car. On the way, she looks out for the chestnut tree in the church yard where she collects conkers in autumn.

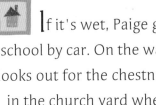

Cidinha's house is between the village shop and the open space where the children play football. Her school is just a short walk away, straight down the same red, dirt road.

At school

Everywhere in the world school is important. While we learn about children in other countries, they are learning about us. A school may have lots of classrooms, books, equipment and a playground, or lessons may take place under trees.

"We are learning to work out how much things weigh while other children are reading and drawing." Paige and her friends started school in the nursery class when they were three years old.

"I like wearing these clothes because they show that I go to school. Not everyone goes to school so I feel lucky, especially when I learn how to write a new word."
—**Cidinha**

Children in Vietnam have to share the school day because there are not enough schools or teachers: Linh goes to school in the afternoons. When he arrives, he does exercises called *duc* with the whole school in the shade of the trees the children have planted.

Linh and his friends plant and water new trees to give shade and protect the soil from floods.

 "I like to be the first in the classroom and surprise the others when they arrive. There are only nine children in my class today because some of them think it is too cold to go out. The temperature outside is minus 42 degrees centigrade! Today we're practising the Cyrillic alphabet."—**Sasha**

"My best friend Jordan and I are using the internet to share news with school children in other parts of Australia. Sometimes we play computer games, too."—**Alexis**

Anusibuno calls herself Mary at school, the same name as her teacher. She helps to sweep the classrooms and the yard before lessons start. She shares her class with younger children, so it's quite crowded. Sometimes her friends don't come to school because they have to help their parents at home.

At Natali's school, the children work on their own, sitting in groups at separate tables. The teacher talks to them one by one. Everyone has a special box with their name on it for their own projects, pens and pencils. Natali enjoys silent reading, and writing stories.

Shakeel wears a blue and white school uniform. Because it's hot and dusty, the children go barefoot. Their teacher wears a traditional sari. In art class, she sits cross-legged on the mats with them. Shakeel is printing with a vegetable called okra. He decorates his painting with dried lentils.

Playtime!

Children all over the world use what they find around them to invent games, try out new ideas, make their own toys and have fun. Some children work hard to help their families. Others have lots of homework. But there's always time for play.

Ludovico, the village where Cidinha lives, is hot, dusty and dry. It has one dirt road, lined with houses made of earth. When Cidinha and her friends play football or their favourite skipping game *elàstico*, they kick up clouds of red dust. They cool off by swimming and splashing for hours in the lake. They don't have toys, but an old bicycle wheel makes a good hoop!

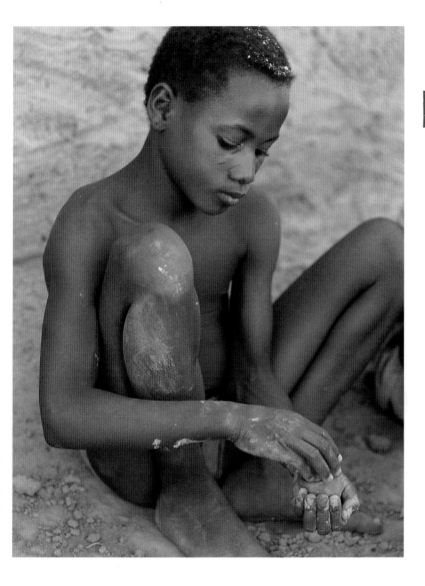

"I play with my sisters and other relatives. There are 18 children living in the same compound, so someone is always ready to join in the fun. We mark out squares in the earth to play hopscotch and make toys and people from clay. We leave them to dry in the sun and then we play with them."

—Anusibuno

"I love Hamish, my hamster. I play with him every day. We also have two goldfish: Freddie is mine and Bug is my sister Bobbie's." Paige likes drawing, too. Her kitchen wall is covered with her pictures.

Shakeel draws tracks for his marbles in the dry, sandy earth. His friends are wearing long, cotton tunics called *kurta* to keep cool.

Like most children in rural Vietnam, Linh has no toys, but makes up his own games. His favourite game is *Vong*: each player uses rubber bands to shoot pebbles at a target. The winner (the person who hits the target) keeps the rubber bands.

"I make houses in the snow. When I work from dawn to dusk, I can almost finish a house in a day. I smooth the walls, inside and out. If the snow is damp and sticky, I make little tables, beds and chairs."— **Sasha**

★ Natali practises the piano with her mother every day after school. She enjoys playing, but she would rather read, or watch videos eating take-away pizza. She has lots of toys, games and books of her own. At the moment, she's reading a book called *California Girl*.

The sun is blazing hot in Alice Springs where Alexis lives. After school, she and her friends ride their bicycles to the pool, or play basketball. Alexis also likes watching television and listening to music.

Helping others

Because we share our lives with the people around us, we have to help each other in all sorts of ways. Doing special jobs for our families is an important part of growing up. Whether we set the table, tidy our toys or look after animals it can be fun to share the work at home.

"Every day, I sweep the rooms and fetch firewood. My sister and I like washing the cooking pots and dishes because when we've done them, they are clean for visitors. They can see how much we help our mother, and we feel proud."—**Anusibuno**

Every two days, Sasha and his brother Vanya collect water from the well. They pull the heavy churns on a sledge. Sasha also clears snow from the path, brings in logs for the fire and helps with the cooking. He is especially good at making meat dumplings called *pelmeni*.

Paige's favourite job is cleaning her hamster's cage. "I like taking care of Hamish: I give him fresh sawdust and water. The job I like least is carrying my toys and clothes back up to my room from downstairs as there are so many stairs to climb!"

Shakeel helps his mother make flat bread called *chapatis* outside the kitchen. He helps his father with building work when their house needs repairs. Shakeel's own job is feeding and milking the goats. When he is older, he would like to do the shopping and carry the heavy bags for his mother.

Linh's special job is feeding rice to the chickens twice a day. His family keeps pigs as well, but Linh keeps away from them because he doesn't like the noise they make!

"Cooking is the job I like best. I mix things and then lick the spoon. That's lots of fun, but I don't enjoy tidying up afterwards."—**Natali**

Alexis helps sort her dirty clothes into whites and colours. She puts them in the washing machine, and then hangs them out to dry in the sun.

Cidinha helps her mother break babassu nuts. The oil in the nuts is valuable because the villagers use it to make soap which they sell. Cidinha can exchange the nuts she breaks at the village shop for a new pencil case or exercise book.

Time to eat!

Every place in the world has its own special food and different ways of cooking and eating that are part of its history. Some of us can choose from many types of food; others eat the same meals nearly every day and hardly ever have sweets or treats. Children everywhere love to eat because food tastes good, and it helps them grow big and strong.

Sasha's family eat their main meal, called *obed*, in the afternoon. They start with soup made from vegetables grown in their garden and then they eat pickled fish, ham, stuffed tomatoes and pastries. They need lots of food to keep them warm in the freezing winter. Sasha's favourite meal is *borsch*, a soup made from beetroot.

In Vietnam, even small children are expert at using chopsticks. Dinner is called *bua toi.* The main part of the meal is rice, with small dishes of fish and vegetables. Linh's family grows rice and vegetables in their own fields. Sometimes they buy pork, Linh's favourite dish, from their neighbour.

Cidinha's family and neighbours crowd into the living room of her house to watch TV while they have dinner, called *janta.* They eat rice and beans flavoured with spring onion and coriander which they grow themselves. Meat comes from their own chickens and pigs. Sometimes they eat fish which Cidinha's father and brothers have caught in the lake.

Anusibuno eats porridge made with maize or millet for every meal. She and her sisters sit outdoors, sharing bowls and eating with the fingers of one hand. She likes *bito*, a soup made with leafy vegetables and nuts which they grow themselves.

Once a week, Paige has her favourite meal of roast meat or chicken with roast potatoes, vegetables and gravy. On other days, she might eat pasta with tuna fish, fish fingers or salads. When Paige invites school friends home for tea, they have chocolate biscuits as a treat.

Shakeel tears *chapatis* - soft, flat bread - into pieces, and uses them to scoop up rice and *dal*, a lentil stew. Most days his mother cooks vegetables in a spicy, curry sauce. Shakeel looks forward to Sundays when they have meat curry called *gosht*.

"I go to my grandmother's house for tea on Friday nights with all my cousins. We eat pasta, and barbecue in the garden. My favourite food is take-away hamburgers. We have them for lunch at school on Fridays, and once a week for tea at home."—**Alexis**

Natali enjoys salads made from the fruit and vegetables that grow in hot, sunny California. Everyone in the family has their own choice of salad dressing and a choice of milk or fruit juice to drink. Once a month, for a treat, they eat take-away pizza which Natali's mother orders by telephone.

Time for bed

At night-time, we rest our minds and bodies before we wake up to another busy day. As evening comes, we start to feel sleepy and look forward to bed, whether we sleep on a mat, in a hammock, bunk or family bed.

"I pretend I'm a martian in the silver pyjamas Mummy made me. She blesses me and kisses me before I fall asleep."—**Sasha**

Shakeel goes to sleep listening to his sister reading stories, or watching TV. He has a favourite pillow which he doesn't like anyone else to use.

Before Paige goes to bed, she reads a story with her mother or father, or plays a game. She cuddles up with her toy monkey and then her parents say goodnight.

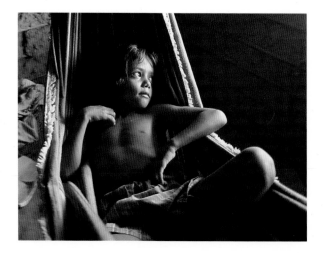

It's hot at night, so Cidinha often sleeps in just a pair of shorts. Before she goes to sleep, her sister or her mother reads to her, or they look over her school work.

"After my parents kiss me goodnight, I go to sleep with my most cuddly bear, Chester Junior." Natali likes to keep special toys and photos around her bed.

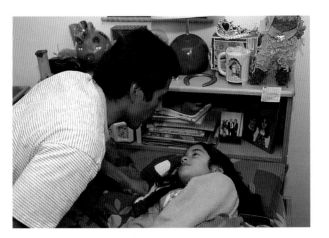

Alexis goes to bed late. "Some nights I have a shower, then I read comics to myself before Mum comes for a hug and kiss."

"I go to bed as it gets dark, when the frogs start croaking. The last thing I do is fetch the pillow and pull down the mosquito net. We don't need a blanket until the morning when it gets cold."—**Linh**

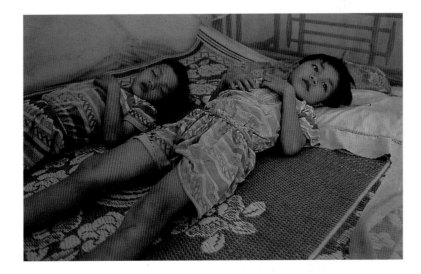

"After supper, my sisters fetch the sleeping mat. We tell each other stories and sing songs as we lie in the dark. I listen to the sounds of animals and people and drift off to sleep."
—**Anusibuno**

In my dreams

Our dream-life takes us to places different from our everyday lives. When we dream at night, we tell ourselves stories while we sleep. Daydreams are what we wish for when we're awake: peace in the world, a visit to the moon, a day at the beach or a new toy. We especially wonder what life will be like when we grow up, and dream about what we will do in the future.

"My dream is to be a vet, and have a horse of my own. I want to fly around the world to see different creatures that live in faraway places. The world might be quite different when I grow up, but I'll always love animals"—**Paige**

"In my dreams, I go into the stories I've been reading and watching on TV. I become part of them, a princess or a character from a film. When I grow up, I want to be like Pocahontas, strong and fast, brave and loyal."
—Natali

 "I never remember the dreams I have when I'm asleep but when I'm awake, whatever I'm doing, I dream of a brand new bicycle, with shiny mud guards and brakes that work."
—**Shakeel**

"In my dreams, our house is turned into the Kingdom of Happiness, where Mummy is queen, my sister is a princess and my brother a prince. I am the head of the Kingdom. There is a singing firebird with sparkling feathers that shine at night."—**Sasha**

"One day, I'd like to be a famous singer and dancer. For now, I wish I could have a doll. Sometimes I dream I'm sitting in the shade by a well playing with a doll; sometimes I dream about the sea."—**Cidinha**

"I often dream I'm meeting the musicians in my favourite band. They sing for me and talk to me. In real life, when I grow up I will travel the world, listening to music everywhere I go."—**Alexis**

"I dream of the day when our house is finished. When I grow up, I want to be a builder like my father. People will pay me to build houses for them, and I will use the money to build a home for my own family."
—**Linh**

"I dream of being a teacher when I grow up, or perhaps a photographer. I'd like to take pictures of ordinary people doing their everyday work, and of children playing." —**Anusibuno**

Ghana

Anusibuno lives in Ghana on the west coast of Africa, the second largest continent in the world. In the south of Ghana, there are cities, forests and farmland. The capital, Accra, is modern and bustling. In the north, where Anusibuno lives, it is dry and dusty. Fewer people live there, and life is slower and more traditional. Many people have to fetch their water from the village bore hole and instead of electricity, they use kerosene lamps and cook over a wood fire. Everyone shares the work in the compound where Anusibuno lives: children help to pound millet and maize to make porridge, and look after animals.

Anusibuno uses an English name at school. She speaks English as well as her own language, Kasena-nankani, because Ghana was once ruled by Britain. Today, all the countries of Africa are independent.

India

Shakeel lives in Hyderabad in India, the second most populated country in the world, after China. Hyderabad is hot, dusty and dry, but other areas in India are green and lush.

Parts of India are modern, with hundreds of factories producing computers, cars and electronics. The biggest cities, Calcutta, Delhi and Bombay, are very crowded. However, three quarters of India's people work outside the cities, on the land, growing most of the world's tea and cotton.

Ancient traditions and customs of different religions - Islam, Hinduism, Sikhism, Christianity and Buddhism - are part of everyday life for most Indians. Shakeel is a Muslim. He speaks Urdu, one of sixteen languages spoken in India. The main ones are Hindi and English.

Russia

Sasha lives in Siberia, which makes up most of Russia, the biggest nation in the world. Although Siberia covers such a large area, not many people live there, because of the extreme cold in winter. Northern Siberia is inside the Arctic circle, not far from the North Pole. In some places, the snow never melts, and even the sea is frozen. Sometimes the cold can freeze your breath.

In summer, people spend much more time outdoors. They grow vegetables and grain on their farms. Sasha's village is well-known for its crops of camomile flowers, which Sasha helps pick to make tea and medicine which the villagers can sell.

Many Siberians work in coal mines, or producing timber from the forests. Others go to the cities to find work. Sasha's step-father works in Novosibirsk, the capital of Siberia.

Australia

Alexis lives in Alice Springs in Australia, the only country that is also a continent. Australia is an enormous island with animals, such as the koala and the kangaroo, that are found nowhere else in the world.

The first Australians were Aboriginals, like Alexis' father and grandmother. In the last century, people from all over Asia and Europe have settled in Australia. They are attracted by the hot, sunny weather and an outdoor life: beaches, picnics and barbecues.

Most people live on the coast, in and around the main cities: Canberra (the capital), Sydney, Perth and Melbourne. Alice Springs is in the Australian outback, the flat, hot, dry, semi-desert region in the heart of the country. The best-known feature of central Australia is Ayers Rock. People travel from all over the world to see this huge outcrop of red sandstone in the middle of the desert.

USA

Natali lives in California on the west coast of the United States of America. The fifty stars on her country's flag symbolise the fifty states that make up the nation. The USA is the richest and most powerful nation in the world. The first people to live there were American Indians. Then ships arrived bringing settlers from Europe. Today, most Americans descended from families who came there from all over the world. Everyone speaks English and, in the southern parts of the country, many people speak Spanish as well, as it is close to Mexico and South America. Natali's father's family is from Mexico, so Natali speaks both Spanish and English.

More people live in California than anywhere else in the United States. It has a warm, sunny climate, where fruit and vegetables grow well, and there are beautiful beaches shaded by palm trees.

Brazil

Cidinha lives in Ludovico village in Brazil, the biggest country in South America. Her home is in the north, near the Amazon river and the rainforest that grows around it. Half the year, it is dry and dusty; the other half, it rains. Sadly, the Amazon rainforest is disappearing, together with its wildlife because so many trees have been cut down. People all over the world are working with the Brazilians to prevent this.

The city of Rio de Janeiro is famous all over the world for its beautiful beaches and its carnival, held every year. Life in the countryside, where Cidinha lives, is quite different. Although Cidinha's family has a television set, the electricity supply is weak, and there are power cuts nearly every day.

Most people in South America speak Spanish, but in Brazil, the main language is Portuguese, a reminder that the country was once ruled by Portugal.

Vietnam

Linh lives in Ky Anh district in Vietnam. Vietnamese people describe their country as shaped like a bamboo pole with a rice-basket at each end. Rice is the most important crop, and everyone eats it every day. It is mainly grown in the north and south of the country, where people live in farming and fishing villages. Linh's home is in the narrow, coastal strip of land in between.

Vietnam has a humid, tropical climate, perfect for rice, which needs hot, wet conditions to grow well. Monsoon winds bring the rain, but they also bring storms which sometimes ruin the rice fields and leave people without food. Where Linh lives, the country is often hit by typhoons, strong winds and floods which destroy houses, farms and animals. At school, Linh helps to plant trees to stop the soil being washed away.

UK

Paige lives in Brighton, a town by the sea on the south coast of England. England, Scotland and Wales make up the island of Great Britain, and with Northern Ireland, the United Kingdom. England is linked to France by a tunnel under the sea.

Britain is a wealthy country. Everyone speaks English, with different accents depending on where they live. Paige's family is Christian, but people from all over the world have come to live in Britain and have brought with them a rich mixture of cultures and religions. Britain is a small country with a big population, and the cities, especially the capital London, are very crowded. In the countryside, life is more peaceful and there is still plenty of green farmland. As it rains in both summer and winter, people often complain about the weather.

MORE MULTICULTURAL BOOKS IN PAPERBACK FROM FRANCES LINCOLN

A IS FOR AFRICA
Ifeoma Onyefulu

This breathtaking photographic alphabet captures the
rhythms of day-to-day village life in Africa in images and words
that will delight children the world over.

Suitable for National Curriculum English - Reading, Key Stages 1 & 2; Geography, Key Stages 1 & 2
Scottish Guidelines English Language - Reading, Levels B & C; Environmental Studies, Levels B & C

ISBN 0-7112-1029-2

I IS FOR INDIA
Prodeepta Das

This photographic ABC captures the spirit of India in all its
diversity, introducing the reader to the rich culture of Indian
life in town and country.

Suitable for National Curriculum English - Reading, Key Stages 1 & 2; Geography, Key Stages 1 & 2
Scottish Guidelines English Language - Reading, Levels C & D; Environmental Studies, Levels C & D

ISBN 0-7112-1101-9

W IS FOR WORLD
Kathryn Cave

A round-the-world alphabet covering more than twenty countries,
with heart-warming photography from Oxfam and simple text
by award-winning author Kathryn Cave.

Suitable for Nursery Education - Personal and Social Development
National Curriculum English - Reading, Key Stage 1; Geography, Key Stage 1
Scottish Guidelines English Language - Reading, Levels B & C; Environmental Studies, Levels D & E

ISBN 0-7112-1364-X